SPRING'S FALL

AUTUMN NUMBERS
BOOK I

SPRING'S FALL

AUTUMN NUMBERS
BOOK I

HARAMBEE GREY-SUN

Cover design by Phillip Gessert
Cover photographs by Harambee Grey-Sun

Published by HyperVerse Books
www.hyperversebooks.com
writing between and beyond the lines

ACKNOWLEDGMENTS

The author would like to give sincere and humble thanks to the editors of the following publications in which earlier versions of some of the poems in this book first appeared:

Erete's Bloom: "He Said (Krystina's Theme)"
RiverSedge: "Audience"

CONTENTS

YEAR SIX

YEAR SEVEN

YEAR EIGHT

EPILOGUE

NOTES

INTRODUCTION

INTRODUCTION

This book is a freak. Possibly a mistake from its very conception.

A long story comprised of forty-six short-shorts, all of them in verse. A concept album in musical words. A postmodern musical on the page. This is an experiment. A frankenpoem. A HyperVerse.

Rejecting the "rules" of what contemporary poetry should be, *Spring's Fall* is unapologetically unfashionable, written in the spirit of the complex-but-imperfect music many of us hear and sing to our insecure selves in adolescence.

Readers will follow Sevin as he ambles around his hometown one last time, reminiscing about the moments that made him into the young man he's become. He reimagines, not only his own thoughts and feelings, actions and words, but also those of the girls and women who made a significant mark on him. The story is told in verse in order to represent the way the mind—particularly the adolescent mind—may work on a subconscious level.

If you firmly believe poems have to behave a certain way, put this collection back on the shelf. If you're looking for a book that abides by the strictest rules of narrative, shut your eyes. If you're expecting poetry falling in line with the current academic fashions, you'll be sorely disappointed. What you'll find here is a rebellious spirit running with and against the inevitable unfairness of life and love.

A poem very much out of its place and time, *Spring's Fall* is not an easy read, but it's not nearly as challenging as growing up.

SPRING'S FALL

AUTUMN NUMBERS

BOOK I

PROLOGUE

SPRING THEMES

Mary or Margaret—
who cares why she's grieving?
White funeral, black wedding—
neither is the place
for a brown visitor in ragged
running shoes, carrying a broken
bicycle on his raw shoulder.

One last look over
where my self-awareness sparked,
near the river's bank at dawn,
the water, reddish green,
sluggish. It can't help but yawn
on the horizon: that giant tyger's head,
vomiting the remains of some lamb,

possibly diseased. Hell, it is not easy
to find enough bites to satiate a family
famished, naked, and housed
in a dumb deity's mouth.
Well, we're all ravished from birth
by Reality.
        But I'm just passing through.

I've rambled by these brambles
many times before,
but never before with a mind
warped by eight years of wars
begun on whitegrounds where
mature thoughts bloomed
and doomed.

Was I a wise general
or just a wiseass,
generally a bum?

One last bruised look,
perusing a human autumn,
reading deep upon a rusty rhyme
when numbered lives fell
to realize God isn't one,
neither is man
nor woman,
nor me, slumbering my way across
his
or her
or whose story?

    I'm just passing through.

YEAR ONE

PLAYGROUNDS

In younger days, way back then,
       I played with Freedom
under bright skies bathed in blue;
       worries peaced, as one.

I recall swinging on sets,
       crawling up steel slides,
hanging from bars for monkeys,
       seek-touch-smile-and-hide.

Merry-go-rounds can spin unevenly,
       or so it may seem, holding too tight.
       While riding, I have to squint my eyes at the sunlight.
The created breeze caresses my face
       as friends of branches serenade me.
       When it stops spinning, my eyes open, what might I see?

In younger days, way back then,
       she loved me dearly—
Freedom led me through vast fields
       to walk, talk, merely.

I recall friends and laughter,
        sun cups, honeybees;
never stung till I left the
        fort under ash trees.

Merry-go-rounds haunt and taunt me in dreams,
        winding in a mind laid like a ground
        grey and played upon by specters reaping those
                                blue sounds.
The pure azure life I lost in years past—
        a blood-blue bubble that just reminds.
        Only youth, or did I leave love for my self behind?

TEN

Sitting on a swing at recess,
after lunch,
I've forty minutes in hand,
but nothing dry I can trust.
I swing back and forth
over an area grass
has long passed, disturbing
the leavings, stirring dust.

I spot my love across the brownground
playing hide-and-seek
with her friends,
all of whom outclass me.
One year up,
she has me bested on age and peers.
Elsewhere, unchosen and unchallenged,
I'm king of reverse cheers;
here,
sweat threatens to freeze me clear.

If I stopped swinging, left my cloud, walked up to her,
would she pause her game, tag me with a sincere smile?
Could I swim in heartening pools, led to by her bloodstream;
or should I stand alone, unrescued, on my dusty isle?

If I left my swing, walked over, and tried speaking to her,
would she understand my mouth babbling,
words bumbling about,
while I wonder what minds like hers dwell on at night
or what desires her classroom daydreams play out?

Respite over, I retire to the tennis court
where my pals and peers of grade five
play their own game.
A game of soccer fails
to turn my mind off what's up,
but succeeds in kicking
some sense out;
turn back to pain…

I leave the sport
and the court
and my friends behind,
stepping back out among
once tense dandelions.
I post myself, lean on
a post near a door, then
I'm startled by the alarm,
charmed into silence
when she breezes by to get in.

If I turned and closed my eyes and counted to ten,
may I start the game over, might she reappear?
Is she picky, careful about with whom she runs around,
or has she a liberated spirit, devoid of fear?

If I drew up some new rules and made up my own find-game,
may it attract an elusive one who wakes like spring's wind?
I wonder what it meant when, as she passed by me,
eyes dropped with a quick glance—
I could swear that she grinned.

LORA'S SONG

Last morning, I entered the woods
        behind the library.
        Scratch marks on tree barks, etched
        on memories, stories for fires…
I strolled along the path by the stream,
        this domain's life vein.
        A babbling brook murmuring with mud in mouth…
        What's it telling me?

I wondered: What can come after Childhood,
        when scenes like these will mean nothing
        more than being lost in a big world?
        I shivered just to think of the loss.
Then, it felt like
        the breeze was blowing me secrets;
        through the leaves of trees, it seems
        I learned of something quite mysterious.
That which turns worlds made my senses go dizzy—
three secrets, I promised I'd lock up with a smile.

That evening, cycling for home,
        I began whistling an anthem.
        A chorus of blue jays and cardinals
        joined in, then carried it from me.

In the distance, the streaks in the sky
     displayed his signature;
     in blinding pink, azure staggers,
     his name painted the heavens.

I've heard of a stage of Life they've labeled "Love."
     It's supposed to make your mind fly insane
     and drive your body to ruin—
     a loss of sight for what's true and right.
I've seen this manifest among adults
     who hallucinate, concentrating on aches
     within the head and the heart.
     Some fall as if pierced by an arrow.
I have symptoms—but pills will cure, swallowed with a smile.

THE TRIALS OF CHILDREN

Illiberal world,
and still some manage to find freedom,
but is it only in their heads?

The young and the old,
feeding on envy of the other
end of the spectrum,
meeting in the unhealthy
green middle.

Carelessly cycling through,
conditioned to withstand any terrain,
my bike and I bounce and weave,
move on our way,
as the immature are apt to do.

Responsibilities
    —well, those are tomorrow's epilogues.

Playing at life,
a girl rich with attention can do that;
a beggar struggles to attain

Freedom of choice—
I choose this road. Forbidden fruit
trees stand at the sides,
my boundaries. This is the street
where the upper classes dwell,
free to engage
in trade of their prized possessions
without any duties.
It's tradition.

I reside on the other side.
Not unlike a tourist from a straight land,
I've come here for a broader view.

Tammys and Sallys skip the ropes, hopscotch
to the rhythm of nursery rhymes.
Timmys and Billys take to trees, retreating to their forts,
defending the end-realms of make-believe…

THE CHILDREN'S RHYME

"Life is entangled yo-yos,
strings of strange jokes with strong punchlines.
Flicks move worlds; worlds collide, twist their twines.
Toy joys—playtime grows to 'Share and Show.'"

The aged look on from their guard posts
on their porches, humming, slightly rocking back and forth,
reminiscing through amber shades—that is, until they see me.

They can't help but focus on
this oddboy too-near their lawns.
Rusty pedals trade noises for their gazes.

> *"Death is an attractive magnet,*
> *a great black wall with white space on the other side.*
> *A grand trick on the Creator is to play seek-and-hide,*
> *but try it and see what you get!"*

Should I try to…no—
       No responsibility.
The trade winds blew
my fate near
when a chestnut bur
hit my ear
and drew blood.

Foreboding:
the rustling of leaves
by no breeze. I wonder
just what more will be drawn

when the runts of the realms
of make-believe descend
with their switches
and swordsticks?

Free to travel,
I take this freedom for what it's worth
and pedal harder,
passing a game of kick ball
transitioning to dodge ball.
The target: Guess who?

The object of stares—
I'm outclassed, out of place,
subjected to fingers,
pointing, accompanied by
giggles and chestnut grenades
tossed by the boy soldiers from their posts.
The girl guardians are worse;
their stinging laughter lingers on.

RAINFALL

Outside windows, the rain seems green, so far away,
even though the drops lightly tap, run down the pane-lanes.
The constant drip—a waterfall in its dying throes,
or a heart wrung till droplets are as steady as throbs, lost.

In an absence of common sense,
I left my shelter, went out
under a sweltered ice-sky.

For the farmers, the rain is such a blessing,
a harbinger of well-fed families, profits, and brighter futures;
for flower gardeners, too, who care first for beauty.
As for me, I could do without external storms.

If it were only rain, perhaps I wouldn't mind so much,
but the harbinger comes with mud and, worse,
                                        deceptive puddles.
Even the leaves fall with the rain, like countless random
love notes tossed away, the inquiries unanswered.

Optimists say, "The rainfall
makes nature's colors more vivid."
But the skies must darken, too.

It goes against all sense—Why do children love to play
in the rain, begging for a later illness

                        to take from their days of joy?
I had an umbrella in hand,

                but it's useless against what the wind carries.
So I returned home to save it for a lighter day.

YEAR TWO

AUDIENCE

Here I stand,
in a mass, seeking order
among the throng
of ticket-holders gathered
around the house the Community built
(with hands connected to collect "the Wills"),
waiting for the presentation to begin.

Here I stand,
behind a fence whitewashed
last week, sullied now
by the passings and
droppings of the days
filled with children's fingerprints
and birds with the good instincts
to stay aloft, flying above it all.

Who will stand and come to usher me inside?
Must there be a change of the guard just to escort me,
one of the plumb luckless to miss out on the "first-come" policy?
Would I count as more, be more valuable, with a new number?
Would I qualify, then, to share laughs,
rather than to duck and dodge them
before I move on?

There they stand,
patiently waiting to be
accepted into the premises
from which we were all once banned.
What was all the fuss and clamor
back then, chatter about
the "Greatest Show" to ever play
this town?

There they stand,
fidgeting, now shuffling in,
bit-by-bit, grabbing programs,
scanning the rows to have best pick
of their position, a grand view
for the opening ceremony,
welcoming the new cast of players.

Will they serve us laughs, drama, mystery?
Will the show feature dances or magic tricks?
Illusions can stretch attentions infinitely.
Mistakes aren't for Masters, such as our new stars,
but for amateurs like me.
Last year, I fell from my stage—silent now,
among the rows, here I sit.

THE CHILDREN'S
MASTER-MYSTERY THEATER

The lights dim. The music begins
and then swells.
Curtains rise to give a clear view
of an affair ready to progress.
"Relax, and know you'll be entertained…"

We sit silently with lips parted,
hands raised to scratch
when the question's put before us,
equalized in our audience:
"For whom does your fate await?"

Instructed to hold off applause
till the last of curtains fall,
we're allowed to watch dramas unfold,
study the actors role-playing
with an actress so near-far
in The Children's Theater.

Kiss quick—one moves along,
lets her break out into song,
spilling a glossy bliss, unbound

when he looked into her eyes,
never betraying his disguise.
He portrayed a Master.

The little dialogue flies too high
for lowered heads.
Their conversation's vain in meaning,
adorned beautifully, but hollow,
like the ring he pushed on her.

The actors swagger without slowing;
backstage…Who knows?
What a wonderful craft to stage here!
The actress is a jeweled tool to amaze,
performing the Jill-of-all-their-trades.

Worn down but sworn to sound,
whirling in her merry way,
she's captured in her own mind.
Sweat beads form and makeup runs,
but without missing two steps or one,
she dons a new mask.

To mark the occasion, curtains fall;
we rise, make a spectacle of our ovation—

a production to behold in and of itself.
As gracious guests, we've shown
we're worthy, ready for the next show.

The players line up, bow,
leave discretely—a hint, leading.
Entranced, most follow our hosts:
Back to the streets. "Die, Unity!
Fight on, self" for a body
that conceals a Master.

PINK EYES

One, young,
aged through the ways of boys and girls,
attitude climbing altitudes—
Experience excuses lines
between ages,
making children rise, wise beyond their years.

Girl, young,
obsessed with unfair fairy tales.
Confused by rings and things shining
"till death…do you…?"

Some may try ice,
some try fire,
many try avoiding these fights
—conflicts pick, for keeping, a few.
Surviving, trying
with pink tears, blue eyes;
chances are *"the fault lies with you;*
some occasions call him to remind."
   "Why should a girl in grade six fuss like a baby?"
        "Why chill a public swaddled in their own affairs?"
     "Real adults brave these fierce flames every day.
       Situations like yours must be too common for most folks to care."

One, young,
encouraged to tell all details,
too close to influence—
Circles of friends refuse less
than lined, dirt-blurred secrets.
"...*grownups don't fear the dark...*"

Girl, young,
in the public's eyes, averts her own.
Dressing, tightly, bruised skin
lest storytime tells small tales on her.

Some may cry rape,
some cry abuse,
many cry less innocent lies
—facts play keep-away from a few.
Blinding herself, crying
with pink tears, black eyes;
rumors say *"shed your tears through;*
none will help fill a bucket of truth."
   "Why claim stolen property to only end up bankrupt?"
          "Why force, rush your first long-living crush into divorce?"
      "'Girlfriend' sounds much better than 'victim, dumped.'
        You're too mature to quit now; you're too good to let it get worse."

HE SAID
(KRYSTINA'S THEME)

He promised not to tell a soul about those secrets of mine,
tales woven with absurd strands,
sometimes mistaken for lies.
He accepted me for what I was,
and more for what I could be
—a conversion administered
by a self-ordained Man.

He warned he had a troubled mind, "so excuse the blackouts,"
some problems stirred up at home
that ran away when he did.
I swore I could help him see through this
based on what I had learned
from my father; but this boy has grown,
and now it's his turn.

Why run to hide and stay? All relationships go this way.
Love has thorns—it hurts. "Sacrifice" is the watchword.
Surviving travails ensures
a happy fever after.
My position's a humble one
…or so he said.

He begged me to look after him; for without me, he's lost.
With no guardian angel,
he could go on to do worse.
My girlfriends have envy-enveloped
their brown–dull, boring lives
—no handholding or promises;
they seek to sever with words.

He thinks I'm too into myself, too often remote;
yet I'm contemplating schemes
to challenge legends I've heard.
Black flags fly freely for anarchy
(I secretly mend one that's white);
I swear I can convert his stalwart soul
after I reform this meek heart.

Victimhood is a must for martyrs for happiness.
How many saints are named who never suffered through pain?
I play the ways of time,
between what's lost and what's mine.
My role's a silent one
…or so he said.

S N O W

"All this will pass."
I read that on a wall
in spray-paint red
on my way
to a day at school,
avoiding snowflakes
created to fall randomly.

Where is God now?
Up in the sky,
I just saw sullen clouds
(resenting those above, us below?)
releasing snowflakes
to fertilize the soil.

There are snowmen and girls who build them,
knowing all too well one day the sun will reign.
There are snowwomen…The boys who build them
guiltlessly commit the same crime,
playing foully
on these bitter snow days.

Cry over snow…?
The handheld bell calls my attention;
still, it's still ringing
in my ears, my bones,
frozen, abused
by the snowflakes
I failed to evade.

What should I say?
The teacher slipped once
and called on her name,
but only silence replied
from that empty chair
she sat in last Friday.

There are snowforts with snowballs to guard them
from the cold and cruel onslaughts of boys and beasts.
Today, snowflakes help cover a plot
dug only last evening for the girl
who left her fort
and fell through the ice.

YEAR THREE

GRADE SEVIN

All I said was, "Thank you for not smirking,"
then she spat into my eye
and said, *"[Blank] you,*
stupid jerkling." Kissed *Bye*
by my last friend
from the six elements.
Welcome to Junior High.

Personalities warped in the summer space.
One goofy girl deranged her interests,
painted her eyes blue,
bought new red boots
for the first steps into Darwin's halls.

On a rickety stage, I spent the months hanging
on a May mourning, assailed by the crickets
of consciousness: Was I never in love
with anybody, just hating everyone
with equal intensity?
There's my summer.

Here's my September
in an old style, skins

disassembling memories
of accumulated friends.
Flakes of happiness.
Orange, brown, yellow
barbs embedded in gossip vines.

Introducing the Patchwork Jerk
conducting a song of sentience
absent of birds chirping, bees buzzing:
Here I am, burnt fashioned, wearing
my mind turned inside out
for this jungled new world.

Let the wars of simple words
continue and leave me
for the dense season's
background scenery.

MY FAULTS

Why must I be blamed for the shambles?
Which of us conceived this microcosm?

Must persecution be perpetual
simply because I wear the face of my father?
My behavior undefined in her mind, I'm confined
thanks to my likeness to a private enemy
who—today, tomorrow—stalks the streets.

Should I be blamed for repelling her boyfriends?
What status is assigned to her spirits?

Must I alone withstand her rants, tantrums
fueled by rage imbibed, blindly,
after a "holy" union ceremony?
Drinks mixed to (she thinks) cure
only ensure suffering.

                    I couldn't care for relating to kindred
             souls that cry out, hurl epithets and blunt objects.
          I just rope-hope one day a snipe of hers will fly
             too high and clip, snip the strings to the life
                she artlessly crafts—Marion's marionette.

Does she think me blind to the favor
shown to the other, older, equaling her in gender?

Sibling rivalry is normal, I've been told;
but I've heard that the guardian in charge
has the responsibility to stand up for peace,
not sit down, lean back
and cheer on.

It may be my fault I'm not a crowd-pleaser,
but must the intimate teasing be so loud?

Why are our normal conversations so thermal,
comprised of commands demanding silence in response?
Since her words have created my cursed world,
I'd better forget to ask questions. Any answers
would only add pollution in the guise of "solutions."

"What if I just stopped caring?" She threatens me
with this and other fiery prophecies long fulfilled.
"My friends warned me you'd turn and lose respect."
I wonder when I leave her world cold
if they are the ones to be flamed next.

SUNSETS

Viewing worlds through realizing (glass) eyes,
my attention's sentenced to endless detentions.
Home-schooled in scatology, coprology,
I tuck the words that'd scrub a soul
deep away.

Pleasant dreams don't come down everyone's pipe.
Growing up, the details get tougher to straighten.
I've fooled my friends—in company, they know the role
of smiles.
"She doesn't drink" (at least, not last night).
Away with keeps.

then when it ends,
some will assault her with questions of "Why?"
What will she think to tell them then?
Reveal, or say it was my fault?
Odds are she'll lie.
She'll fall back on that *"divorce"* excuse.
On her tear, it keeps the truth out of her views,
out of her mind.

Reared as a man, so I don't play with tears.
Proper parenting: one doesn't show his feelings.
This is a life—spending nights locked in a room,
voluntary. The halls aren't haunted, but still scary.
Hear silent screams.

when it begins,
washed up on wishes, hopped up on hopes, try to fly
beyond her eight clouds. Red mist falling,
passing off a life amiss.
Autumn sunsets
inspire me to reach, grab for a god…

                    Praying (crying) salts the wounds.
              The weather seasons my thoughts.

Lush-living singled a wife;
firewater chalks one score.
Poisoned drinks blackened one life;
scratch the board of yet one more.

KAREN'S SONG

Seeing the odd, pushed from odder numbers (a minor tragedy),
blind-finding friends (oddities added) makes for even comedy.
This lone figure, divorced from those laughs,
brings a morbid pleasure to the sad.

He saw me,
an observer displaced from her time,
under the spotlights of honeyed rays,
sitting, watching the awkward dance
of a boy, tripped up, swerved from his balance.

Back-and-forth
lean other figures in this setting
depending on the mood, on their dreams.
A character lost in a play
noticed me despite instances in-way.

Though considered as a nice one, my heart bleeding a steady flow,
no weeping or words for this one, just curiosity to know
if security exists within
those who function as shadows-in-skin.

I've maintained
my distance as a student of life—
listen to, look at, don't interfere
in the straight paths of the depressed,
lest they turn, unleash feelings long repressed.

Joy and mirth—
delicacies reserved for the few,
once thought to be served warm to all youth.
Who was greedy? I shouldn't care;
won't be there when he's shot by Heaven's stares.

SHADE-CHANGING SIDES

So, they've already counted me out,
out of battles I've hardly engaged.
Shall I exercise my right
to retreat back to the shelter I left?

What is all that talk of "rights"?
Just who bestowed them on whom?
My only option, they say, is "to lose."

Was it my right to be thrown in
the fool-drowning Clowns' Pool,
the bleary eye of the Children's War
initiated by their guardians?

One young man, one aged dream:
reaching the apex of life.
Some declare these years are the best—
yes, for the worst among the lines.

Whipped by water and winds, my muddled
mind managed one clear: taking control.
Here is my freedom, here is my right:
choosing the weapon with which to fight.

Why were we born into green sin
only to rust, begin again? Leaves of weeds—
could they be stainless knives?

Parents, teachers, and peers around,
each seeking hold over
the destinies of other bodies,
losing self-control, are gaining souls—

No choice: A next world waits there for me
somewhere beyond their cares,
where the innocent freely choose to suffocate
or be corrupted by polluted airs.

CHAMELEON

As a shamed chameleon too angry to stay
    among foliage well into its dull age,
I'll remove myself from corridor walls,
    leave a kissed wish for the winds to blow them down.

Books scrunched to the chest, shoulders hunched, head bowed,
    preventing one from getting pushed off course—
Of course, that method of hall-travel is fine for those
    who go through wanting nothing but to find the end.

Me, I've decided, next year, I'll find a new axis, a fresh vine,
one with fruit destined for wines, leaves of colors besides brown.

Like a blameless chameleon
wandering, unnamed, onto a stage
frequented by popular images,
narrow minds (please-easily blindsided),
remembering whens spent as a mime,
one member of the darkened audience,
I will conform to the attitudes of the day,
under spotlights, playing styles;
a lasting master of mind-games,

                           gambling on…

YEAR FOUR

SHAWNA'S NEW WORLD

See
what I saw through travel-weary eyes
upon my high-quiet arrival,
an outlander in a village
shrouded by a mist unnatural
that diverts sight outside, crooking;
and inside: a world unto its own.

Low
among ages, soul fully grown,
I have seen and been places
regarded legendary in this quaint town.
Still, to help this young one belong,
stand tall downhill, I'll play
naïve, or with one well-living the role.

The mist reflects what's within, averting visions from sites beyond;
confusion, thoughts running circles, is the norm, feature of culture.
My appearance alone has been enough for curious stares.
Rubes gape. Red rubbernecks snub
                    ...on, I walk. Erase...

Strange
that, where I come from, diversity
is a rule, as is ruckus;
noise pervades the environment.
Here, we came for a new life, peaceful,
a place to raise children
up right, up from anarchy.

He
took my attention the first day,
and held it for weeks after,
standing out from the dense masses.
A rebellious spirit floating,
detached from their institutions;
a goal I've set to reach, grab in my time.

On survival, standing upright, I know enough:
all young ones must fight;
so some form tribes, little nations—establish names, reputations.
As the two few of our kind, I have determined we be as one…
for his sake,

          not so much for mine.

AN ONYX FOX, PASSING

"Between us:
call us Chronos,
Makers of time—"

Locked out—her time,
my turn; a broken clock,
constructed to be
bendable but dependable
(like clownwork), made me
voiceless in the matter.

What would I want
with this would-be
Bride of Hyde
with the briar patch on her head?
We went out as a joke, me
with my hand on my throat.

"You're too cool to light this fuse?
Is a brother a sister's keep
or—"

Shawna, a black bomb, a breaker
of language, wrangled me from
a few paces away for another date.
Took by a baitless hook from deep
within her eyes (once upon a time,
hazel or caramel, now bloodshot
and swelled). Well, what the heck.

Our second one-hour developed
into the dirty-thirst of a month
drained of liquid poses
from the present: a plastic flower
able to squirt firewater—
a gimmick used to flirt
with the matters
of serious commitments.

"Clearly, you fear midnight."

Not fear. Stark repulsion
at those who'd deign to design
numbers on a clock
and pretend two different are the same.

More than enough meetings, time to propose
we now become shy friends, untying ends
of ruddy, broken bands (so many)
combined to make rubber balls
that couldn't stay put. And that was
the white day she dyed
our florid affair
by spilling some fine lines:

"Reps rub off. I'd long guessed
beneath that stained denim hide
lives a heart dying from being apart
from another, a scratchy lovematch.
I've known your type despite the mangy disguise:
A courteous, nice boy concocts rebellious side
but really a geek,
once 'Student of the Week,'
an amateur actor…a tough guy
sticking it only to his own kind.
I know you have faults; I have a few, too—"

A dum-dum remark, much like saying "blue is blue."

"—but you and I are one, or none.
The dust of crushes brushed aside

inspires sneezes, diseases,
two numbers go in, coincide
suicide."

Among mimes, nameless,
emerged the hometown kid
who sometimes made bad puns
(and some quite good ones):
An unfunny running joke,
trusting the winds' rush to wash off
the aura of convenient love,
in all its humor and horror,
which causes first relationships to end
in laughing, coughing,
and begin choking.

THE FIRST HUNT

Wearing on me, the nits,
        gnats swarming, nipping,
gnawing,
        growing on my conscience.

One of civilization's grey discontents,
                therefore I think
I don't much like alike.

The sustenance
of convenience
is the same as swallowing
my own vomit; a cannibal
              self-rejecting
me and her together—

Who cares for her threats? Forget
the humor and the horror,
I have a hunger, an inner thunder
suggesting: Thread the bitch's lips,
stitch that wound shut...

Her incessancy.
How much was I to take
before collapsing? On too long,
I've gone, an emaciated wolf
who almost too late self-debated:

What sated mortals, by name,
have willingly suppressed,
enslaved their natural appetites?
Am I to be blamed, ashamed
of what my stomach, my nerves
can't tolerate? Nonsense.

There's the fence. Count
the white rabbits leaping…
So what if my tastes differ
from prescribed diets? How
much longer till nighttime?

Perhaps, the gnats say,
I should just take a leap now,
follow them down into neither-
Heaven-nor-Hell's hole.

SHANNA'S SONG

My life here among dry-mouthed peasants
(idol-worshippers who've lost faith in self)
is like a queen's in a bondman's plain land,
tossing bread as her horse trots by.
My entourage, which is sixty
strong, defends and fights for me.

My boyfriend is among the elite,
running plays and passing some off.
I touched down on a goal last autumn
when I accepted his pass at me.
We're leaders of two close-knit cliques;
some have the nerve to hint mine's not deserved!
Facemasks, makeup, and mystery—
No avoiding what's called "hearsay."

Coming home to show off my crown, I'm warned for riding too high;
but being banned, if done again, seems harsh just for flirting offsides.

My parents warn about animals
wild in the fields of bloodstained soil.
They butt heads and clash egos nightly;
woe to the objects of their desires!

If an interception serves my purpose,
I'll toss my scarves to the winds.

My girlfriends chant the fight song with me.
For war, peasants pleasantly wave on.
We lead the cheers as well as the jeers
against the unfortunate ones.
By image, we teach good behavior;
the uncivilized, how to be our tools.
Excluded from our class, they still follow
the rules of our virtual school.

Some say we've the power to rally at our fancy;
but I've heard I, alone, am "oblivious to the days' passing."

THE SYSTEM

If this country's next leaders rule these schools,
congregating by lockers to keep cool,
planning futures where most won't have their say—
ignored, but appeased on those special days
with wet-noodle votes
for presidents, puerile regimens,
and the clubs comprised of their cronies—then,
hard sciences, burn!
The Group System is all one needs to learn.

THE ANTHEM

Players with pigskins, leaders of rallies;
boys and girls passing basketballs;
male and female swimmers and
softball and baseball players
—all perfect pairs, natural.
Guys and gals carry, swing the same rackets;
wrestler knights and mat-maids tumble around.
One pearl to take away
from this netherworld of grade eight:
"It's neither your height nor your weight;
what counts is not how you look,

how you sound or what you do,
but who is around you."

Key turned—clique. Lucky looks locked behind doors.
Nervous sweat: New colors seep through the pores
as memories are churned. I can't cherish,
I can't erase, but the past will perish
and arise remixed.
Phoenix from the grey, flies, burns blue skies bright.
Dawn's attire donned. On the yard, new light:
Find it by the track—
bet the name, leave the realm that's soul-lonely black.

MOVING DAY
(SHAWNA'S THEME)

It's Saturday morning. Some birds and sunshine deign to play so low
on a day when spirits may be raised by such a sound-and-light show.
I tape up my last box. Mom writes "breakables," hands it off to dad.
Looking once more over the grounds of the parting party we had,

I pass my two little sisters
cartwheeling, jumping, running around saplings,
chattering like monkeys about boys they'll meet.

Childish ideas will pass one day;
like families, they'll move away
to take root in new lands and proceed to grow,
                                              strangle another childhood.

Those who come after me may find
it's better to leave toys in mind;
out in the open, enticing...
                    "Nice" boys won't ask, but promise to be "good."

We're off in the car,
            bidding farewell to those waving from their lawns.
My waves are half-hearted. My sisters keep talking.
                    My mom just yawns.

Dad mumbles about his new job while mother reassures us all
of the new friends I'll make once I tear down
                                        my frowny, tight-lipped walls.

Soon, we turn onto the highway,
running west, heading for what older men with
gleaming eyes once dubbed "undiscovered country."

What waits for me, or do I care?
Most kids don't want to play games fair.
I've outgrown dollhouses;
                        missing a plane, such homes, standing, invite the bold.

Boys, play your war-games till the day
sets; by then, I'll have moved away
and used this fragile frame
                                to construct an impregnable fortress of gold.

YEAR FIVE

MUD,
NAILED TO THE CROSSROADS

Head impacting glass ceilings,
brained—teeth digging cell floors—
spear the freshman's eyes and ears
to stained reflecting walls—

Made to look accidental,
this hypercubed creature,
brisk air frisking, arresting
its too-fluid spirit.

    Out of a muddled mind will come green flesh, alien
            to the grinning minutes
          —the clownwork flashes by
   down cobblestone sidewalks,
       up weedy paths never tread,
    leaping undead spring's leavings,
               clearing abstracting thoughts,
     passing birds cussing on bridges,
     burning fuses to autumn bombs—a boy,
     scabbed black, his wind-kissed skin
ticking...

Just off of Golgotha Road—
cramped up, doubled over—
teasing forgotten seeds
with sweat—not one damned tear—

I can see at hyperspeed,
weaving around pebbles,
stalks shooting up, their colors
redding away the brown.

An autumn mood weighing me, seeing visions of spring
unhinged, too many red flowers.
What can it mean to me,
boiling my very nature,
bloodscreaming beyond sound barriers?
I just want to stop, dry out,
scratch the itch, escape the skin—but,
no. The shape's not ready
yet. I look at the future, and
again keep training,
grinning back.
Unlimited play…

IN CIRCLES
(SEVIN'S THEME)

The race of my people: Yellow-black peers running treadmills,
slaves treading waves, too scared to yell for help, for a line
from fellow travelers in this mad rush for glory alone.
      Who snaps the red tape first?
         Who grabs the coveted ribbons?
            Who cares if slugs die in the sun?

      I can't make long distance solo.

         Pass the baton from hand to hand; hand-
      to-mouth, not a breath to spare
   for apologies
or an exhausted catchphrase.

    What is this phase I now pass through,
      jumping hurdles and high bars clear,
         passing all who pause to kiss the ground?

      Hesitance, humility—
     two old friends, hindrances to me.
Could more experience foster my endurance
to survive the distance long running…?

Quest survival: Like games where rats and cats compete,
men and women (of course that runs vice versa, too)
run in circles, like opportunity and the world spin around,
pushed by open lies, making travelers ditzy,
light in the head, lead in their feet.

       Sand traps at track meets—
       pitfalls
—not unlike boxes of sand
kittens use
to sink three foolish mice.

Swear on my future
face, this man'll leave them
blind to any sure trace.

Second winds of energy
inspiring visions: me, hurtling
      past the line that marked the end of Hell.

Night to day, not too long ago,
     her gun fired, releasing smoke—
        the baton now held firmly in his hand—

                relayed to me—

victors meet
in circles.

F E L I C I T Y

THE YOUTH GROUP'S PRAYER

"We go through this world craving Truth,
feeding not on fruits, but on Roots.
May Your high Spirit impregnate revolutions;
living-dead kids reborn—God's human solutions."

Classic tales don't fall worse than this:
Repellent boy charms girl with kiss—
it's better if she's in distress,
and best if lonely or depressed.

From my hill, looking down the grounds,
I spy giggling girls all around,
some fickle and some truly shy,
but most selling themselves for guys.

I praise the Lord, He saw me first—
identity reborn, rehearsed.
No matter how smart or secure,
when men near, women are unsure.

I've sworn true to devote what I
have to God, not to just one guy.
But we all need a respite, fun,
from fishing in punishing puns.

Silent circumambulating
paints pictures of me (rosy rings)
in rituals discarded, past
times long ago with feasts and fasts.

Nights and days alone, in my gown—
white, soft as a graceful swan's down—
I have pondered the waves of fools,
as now, by this reflecting pool…

I cannot travel back in time
to find one boy, repair his mind.
To repent, I torch what is wrong:
those guys with themes, these girls with songs.

Today, not a warm syn with "gay,"
to be happy, fire God's clay.
We're born to charitably live:
take worn souls, cast off, freely give.

SIX SHADES OF HAPPINESS

Some standard love songs contain this promise:
To you I devote my soul with this Kiss.
Heard enough lyrics
and I've read plenty of poems
without ever

finding the real point: Expressing love true.
These clichés on crutches can't near what's due
the one who stands off
all by herself, pondering
some whatever.

I remember her—someone I knew in times younger
when wealth was determined by Freedom,
not associates, decorations.

She was one of the few I could engage in discourse
on topics serious, lost to those
caught up making their declarations.

I digress just to join, make a point clear:
Words fit for her can't be heard in men's ears.
A sight to leave blind,

to behold, artists could try,
but would never

capture her true beyond glitter observed.
How rare to find innocence so preserved!
I know what I seek:
Felicity under trees
or wherever.

MEETING IN THE WILD

I'm asking for an ideal exchange,

                rational, honest.

This must be new for you,

                one so used to changing shades.

I've followed your course: persuaded to forceful.

                What's become of you;

                are you now just a team player?

You've followed a path, lonely; why not quicken your pace,

                walk with me by my side?

The team's uncommon with me, I can assure you.

My marks are higher now than at any time since grade two.

Marks on oral tests—I am sure you score well.

Dates may be your strong aid in points,

                but with respect to history, your mind is spotty

                on the facts, details that soil the earth.

I don't breathe for missing myths,

                kneel by beds, compose wish lists,

                but of minds, I know

                when they've their own sweet tales.

I've secrets unexposed,

but there're none that have a trail you would care or dare to follow.

Remember: We met by the swings back in grade three—

I asked you for a push; you shoved me out of the seat.
I was young—
and still are, playing games of catch.

I've seen tricks played upon the dumb
who wouldn't speak out on the harm done to them.
                        You stab me dead in my chest,
puncture unbroken skin for the sins of men
unrelated to me in wit, personality?
I beg you only watch, washing with fresh ideas—
                        me, the solvent for your thoughts.
Me, as spectator? Your behavior will improve for play
(making him the object I desire in my menagerie).
Promises ~ vain vases.
Then fill them up with truths.

HELL IS HAPPINESS

What the muddy hell is happiness
but a dung hill
built up with guesses
about gods
put together
to get some stinkin' love,
a little warmth? It will also pass
like unnatural gas,
like those childish hopes
of giggling ghosts
hosted by the heart.

A shy boy, imagine,
playing with toys in a bubble
bath of foreign blood, laughs
and laughs as it sinks
into his skin and mixes
with his fragrant essence,
his own odd type.

Now see me
and what is coursing through
arteries and veins

—blood, or breezes
vaporous, condensing
like countless kisses?
This is new,
neither red
nor blue
nor purple
but possibly blonde…

The audacity of me
having no philosophy,
just thoughts that theorize…
She sits, turns her head,
discerning rights from wrongs
crossing her path—eyes still,
whirling mind.
                    I winked.
She turned once more
                    and ran
—but I noticed she smiled.

I have learned,
despite what a girl may say
in classrooms concerning purity,
they prefer guys who've ventured out,

punctured self-doubts,
tracked prey in the fields
like a real hunter:
killer, skinner,
griller, and diner.

As for her,
what will she do
when I stare and say,
"I'm spending six summer weeks upstate
to run the rain-tortured trails.
I expect you'll wait."

Something within me tells
          she will wait
or possibly follow.

YEAR SIX

DUAL MISSIONS: SUMMER VACATION

All set to sing
a song of six pants
and how to wear them,
turning a girl's casual glance
into lip-licking stare,
when I get a cramp
and remember track camp
isn't about scoring
but training
the brain to forget
bitching Cassie, itching Jessie,
pissing Katie, snarky Janet,
suspended Jade, and
suspicious Felicity.

I need to become faster,
ripping time and space, cloning,
multiplying my success.
So I stuff my duffel bag
only with clothes I need
and head for the Greyhound.

I'm drowning in children's
charities, a sea of promises
cried by guilty me after one
wine-dished Sunday.
And now I have to deal,
volunteer Christian cheer
in the face of whining
fat-brats,
teaching techniques
on how to play the waves
to snotty Timmy, cursing Sally,
unholy Betty, tattling Holly,
and their stinking parents…
The worst. I need saving.

God, give me patience
and a dash of brilliance
to survive these summer days
that are predicted to draw on
with a heat unmatched
except, maybe, by Satan's playground.

One big, beautiful discovery:
I think freer
when my freaky heart speeds.
Then I see her,
another beautiful discovery:
hazel eyes; cherries;
skin, white-chocolate dipped…
I swear I'll have her
by the time this first night's dinner ends.

One break in spiritual physics:
A water-walk
by the one who saved me
before I talked
about things like "spiritual physics"…
Greek-god's physique—can't
believe my own boyfriend
didn't tell me he'd
be here. Lucky-stuck, till summer ends.

CHARYNN'S SONG

Between the lines drawn white,
across black asphalt, burning,
                    but tolerable,
it seems I slide with the breeze,
passing others with ease
                    —it seems.

It's all in the form: my strut,
            the arch of my back, arm-pumps.
                        The feet never lead me.

What do I need with a cool theme?
A hot song is just as good,
easier to change each time I
            burn 'em,
celebrate tears of defeat,
watch the weeping
                try to douse the flames.

Equal footing at the crack;
from that point, the other girls only see my back.
They may as well be spectators standing off my field.

No hurdle's
lip will trip. All this talk
of barriers—glass, wood, and brown brick—
is old school. My obstruction tools
are geared for sound, light, space and
any and all colorful matters.

The foul winds they blow behind my back,
        they can stop
                        and watch me bend…

From here, there, and wherever they come:
opponents seeking my competition
            (well, not mine, but that of a mythical woman).
Tightening the spikes in
my shoes, I can't help but to grin.
            They mistake their numbers for added strength.

No hurdles
will serve to swerve me off balance,
whether robed with snake skins
or other scales to tip,
        shine and blind me.
I've come to know

other games they play
and raspy rules
by which they say
      "win" or "lose."

Might be nice to have allies;
but, one-on-one, face-to-face—

              I just take pride in my race.

BYE-AND-BYE

Confronting the haze, into the mist, after running
foreign thoughts through home-memories,
what an unsettling cool-down…

Out, finding myself up, away in a state,
a more conscious mind found its way to mine.
Wandering in a daze, wondering of darker days,
enslaved to the ways of their world,
in my pursuit of happiness, I stole a license for dominance.
                Sun-done.
                Should I sell the same to her?

Approaching in shade, tone, appearance—
at first, I was suspicious of the fairer clone.
"Unselfish love is just a myth," I puffed
only to find she bluffed less subtly.
Survival of the fastest—our philosophies matched;
check mind, body. Now what of our souls?

Plenty of time to discover
while, from the spotlights, I recover
in the shade, turn over a leaf left to itself.

Farewell to my liberty;
the biography is shackled in chains.
Whoever sold me into slavery
received gold from the history
of me chasing Freedom till poor.
Greetings to my destiny;
my reputation's forgotten its name.
If I ever stand before my father,
I shall have no silver honor
for Jill-jacking. Pluck out the core.

SEPTEMBER, FAR FROM THE HARVEST

I'm still having a hard time
with all of these simplicities:
When we...Who's she...Will he...?

Patience is a virus
of the blind self-
destructive who don't mind
living day-to-day, dying
for pity from those
who don't really matter.

The seasons clutch us firmly
in their wormy clichés:
We can die, then squirm
for the dumbest reasons.

What's a boyfriend who bends
from autumn, dismissing me
to read skins he has to know
will dull, end up as kindle?

Hell, let him have the skank in the red bikini;
the dunce saved me once, but I would be damned silly
to stay enslaved to romance; I have a duty
to save my own soul for eternity.

         "Welcome,
to our new school year." With that crooked, smirked return,
Sevin looked like he wanted to fight—or bite—me.
"How was your—?" "Sorry—no time for blind distractions."
Or blonde attractions. What seasons change…

          How deranged…

I've heard of a one-drop rule,
but I can't follow
    every piped song.
Nectar on lips and tongue…
    Can I or can't I
resist swallowing,
swiping grapes,
shying them
of their skins to make my own…
     indulging my
       habitual sin?

If the soul is progressive,
never repeating,

how can I live seeing
        deceiving
my own body with images
of me ever-drowning,
never standing, revolving?
        Eventually
I'll have just one last chance.

After History class, I glanced, shined the shyest
  smile and asked. He passed by with "I still hate to dance."
"*I know. A pretty swift hand of sleight must have tagged…*"
He paused. "*She's in hiding, confusing games,*

                    but me…

Apologies for, last year, being such a girl,
  now I need help learning about our fading world."
He finally accepted, with two promises:
"*It's not a date. No games.*" " I don't count beyond three."
Premature declarations are like purple grapes.

NOTES FOR A DREAM

I had no idea the public library had been remodeled
to look just like your house, the best cubbyhole for studying,
just like your bedroom. *Confused?*
No—it's a nice ruse.

Don't be so quick to budge,
I think I may be sick,
in definite need
of your help,
and privacy.

You don't say,
and I don't play. Not
anymore. *It's not a game,*
not anymore, not this present,
the future, or our past. I have
trouble, I think, with my mind.
I can read the words, hear the lectures fine,
but my notes, when reexamined, are confusing.
Your notes are straight as a…
Fuse? *A spear*
…like the one that pierced the side
of our Savior.
                    Let's just read.

❖

You know, I know of girls who turn pages;
you, maybe, have been torn by one?
Coming of Age undone, she just turns the next—
You know, some say nature is a symbol,
all of it just a sign of schemes
dreamed by a drunken rhymer.
Meaning? I know what you're trying.
Your thoughts, too free. Turn your full attention
to the matters of other fooled brothers' history.
I'll only write if I can fetter my thoughts
to the letters, black in these books.

❖

I don't understand. Why all this focus on tones and shades?
I've come to view all men as trekking from a common place.

Fantastic trees, in your mind, may produce no shade,
but the common ancestor myth isn't one
that will let you pass in any legit class,
only those held on Sunny Days.

❖

Equality under umbrellas: Women and men, on a common crusade,
hand-in-hand, dispelling chaos by spelling the Words of Light:
Stars as Letters.

Reality beyond rainbows: Hand-to-heart,
                                        there are different plans,
and history has told the tale, stomped the trail,
                                in muddy waters, bloody tears:
From man to man,
and woman.

❖

    At the crossroads
again this day
                    and you may
        turn which way?

    In the past, they've unkindly kindled
                        or been "enlightened."
    In the future, they're just ashes
                        and smoke.
        So, in the present,

maybe one of none,

      maybe disoriented this day,
    I will go on
    finding My Way.

CHARYNN'S POSTSCRIPT

His last letter arrived today,
battered and torn…more of a note, pictureless
postcard he could've picked up anywhere.

No explicit indications
of what he's feeling,
or on whom.

The mail carrier couldn't even bear to face me.
He left it in the box, then my hound gave chase.
Without a second glance, he just ran away.

I read the ending first.
It was signed "Sincerely."
What a change!
What of "My Dearest"?
What of "My Love"?

He wrote to reminisce about a sweltering summer spent in the shade.
He wrote of the new school year, the new acquaintances he's made.
He wrote forecasting his best season in performances to come.
But there was no hint of him coming to visit,
no invitation for me to do likewise.

"Sincerely" marked the first and last note
I could trust to tell the underlined truth.

I'd sent him gifts to wear
and some to share between us.

Save for a farewell kiss, foreshadowing,
the currents of our exchange flowed one way
unless one would care to count
the careless scratch he floated my way,
passed off, written off.
Sanity check
destined to bounce.

Who could count all the days unsummed he has strolled in the shade?
Who could count the times I let my guard down and got played?
Who could count the years of a woman too wise for these games?
Well, whatever the hidden number,
the esoteric paths of men will tear on.
As for this one, longing for Freedom—
He can steal his. I've earned mine.

There was no postscript to say.
It was in the stench and stains
of the sincere sweat
that smeared his signature.

YEAR SEVEN

SICKER

Dressed down in white,
              presenting words you might hate to hear,
I have come, this night, bearing a package
              you must take up, unwrap,
and accept as your own
fate tied in tow, in line with mine.

I fear my time,
              if married
to my patience,
              is short.

They crawl beneath my skin,
              scurry,
       tying my nerves,
              stabbing, trying
                     my stability.

Some thoughts have resolved that any cure
       that could correct could only be effective
              by slicing through.
That would only scratch the surface
              as far as others
                     in the skull are concerned.

Churning—regurgitating
> *—spurning—me purging (hating)*
myself of myself—
tell me, tell Him—
> *What can be left to burn?*

These jitters, chilly spells,
> *they come*
more frequently than the winds.
> *Hung-out,*
> *dry eyes…*

> *I'm losing the talent to tell myself my past,*
> *my identity, dreams, tall wishes*
and tales of other times…

I recall: A martyr to human passion
> *or some virgin*
held down in high fashion.

A malady maybe incurable
—but He swears the dead will rise.

> *Care for it, care for me*

You and I
  bound
    in sacrifice.

TO THE ARENA

My life began as a dream
        fading into mind and view.
I say a dream, but perhaps a vision
        would better describe what has transpired
        around me and within me; behind and
        before me, I can imagine nothing
but the omnipresent clear waters, blind-cure,
        developing pictures moving through my mind.

As I grew and dwelled on growing,
        the past and future urged, attempting to merge.
Ever-never was there a tense present
        save for the dream I spent wondering:
        when on earth, when in the heavens,
        when below the flow might I wake up?

My life, as I see it, sees me as a pawn
        to wage battles as plays and sometimes wars as games.
I say some of this to laugh,
        but none of it is meant as a joke,
        unlike festivals and carnivals
        plagued by acrobats, clowns, and cannibals

who feast on the flesh of humorless boys,
    planning to stretch the skin for a tent at the next sad circus.

And how to define "sad"?
    Perhaps as "insipid," "vapid"..."devoid of cares"?
    Or is that "contentedness," "bliss"?
Recurring dream—it is my life in a loop,
    untied and bowed
    in the rapids of not-so-honest airs.
    May my torn life evaporate so all may share.

❖

Days upon days have passed by me,
days I was scared to scream lest someone hear, see
and point fingers, stare under the glare of sunlight;
so I gathered and held to release it all once upon a night.

❖

Not long after my eyes close,
    moments I could not count,
I step behind silken veils,
    parallel lines on the sand.

I've come here several nights past
      for visits long and short.
The changing waves of high tides
      erase the lines in my mind.

Through a haze I enter into
      a tunnel…no…a crowded…
           fashion mall
             …filled with strippers?
      Peripheral sight failing…

Through blurred vision, I seek to capture the forms
before and around me, to give shape, to give meaning,
to define…Unnaturally narrow, my sight in these halls
sees it isn't as plain as I had assumed and thought.
Bumping and stumbling into and over objects I can
not make out, dare not stop for or study;
for if I turn my head (my peripheral vision is dead),
I risk being detoured from my objective, inching closer—
I humbly bumble along, wishing, thinking of my prize
(and wishing, whittling a walking stick to aid my failing eyes).

My dreams, you see, always reward me in a fashion,
in some manner, whether with knowledge of foresight,

or wisdom of insight. Understandings of future, present,
even past events have been made clearer in the journeys
down these lines, these halls, or corridors. The track-trick
of the game is to survive the naming of names;
for if I wake too soon, all would be for naught, you see.
The message is not digested until the wake-up morning after.
In this current state of affairs, I can only fail to comprehend.

Except, I understand this: There is danger ahead.
In all my nightmares and dreams (no distinction necessary),
there is always a climax involving a death, that of mine
or a foe's. So, you see, it is not as a class where one enters
and sits and receives a lecture on the intrinsic value of
one's real life. Esoteric teachings are never passed on
without an initiation, brutal and bloody, weeding out
the unhealthy. Not every man can digest the meal made just for him.
But I've come to fight for the truth and survive, not by my own
determination, or for my own reason, but because I was summoned
by the Stealer of Souls.

I draw my sword (conceived in thought, sharpened in mind),
but, behind and beneath, back deep in my brain, keep it sheathed;
for in these halls, only I may feel pain.
But I keep it, subdued in the subconscious, my last resort
of abortion if my walking stick grows and slows,
keeping me creeping.

A room at the end of these halls—I,
a changeling assuming the role of a beggar,
defensive in stance, hesitant with a glance…
Going on, even if, in the end, I might die.

❖

The endroom is white, blank sheet,
        blinding, or a phase, portal
transporting me through comfort,
        shoving me onto a street.

Past and future merging, I said
        before, not unlike my thoughts
stirring a brew in my head,
        on this street, blacktop with no yellow dots.

A one-man pride-parade of which I am the feature,
the object of the attentive eyes lined up, on guard.
Darkened faces, staid. Draped in brown or soiled orange.
Hands hanging by their hips, restrained,
balled in fists, or crossed behind their backs.
My nervousness, I try to hide.
My lips manage a mangled smile.

My arms limp up like clay-laden tentacles
to make waves. They return a steady stream
of rocks, bottles, and other articles unknown.
My full knowledge of their origins is missing,
but that is something they are not.
After stuttering surprise, I cower for some seconds,
                then dodge for a few more.
But to hold and withstand is unhealthy,
        knowing not till the fall when one can stand no more.

Always and again, in these dreams falls a pattern:
I am often the target of scorn
        for reasons of which I'm unaware.
My neck is tight, still dim-sided in sight
        and, choosing among choices,
                flight takes precedence over fights.

So after a rapid barrage of returns
to the blurred beings on either side,
I take off to jog (to sprint's just a wish).

I hear them, not knowing defeat, pour into the street
and give chase at a pace much more envied than mine.

I've been along this route before;
a re-run, I know a detour.

Now feeling their huffs and their pants,
I trade them only a poor glance
and, with a leap,
        I throw myself above and beyond them.

There was a hill below on the street I'd just known,
and my flight, for a moment, takes this incline.

But from somewhere, something takes a hold of this spirit
I thought was mine
and reverses the gravity of this world,
this unlawful universe in my mind.

Up, straight vertical, up I float…
or fly? I don't know. For the speed
steadily increases, leaving me unable
to gather my thoughts, in pieces.

I know the clouds defy;
they each stay their own course.
Billowy dense, mild fog, light mist,
they descend in rank, these clouds,
while I ascend into space

                —but hold! What is—

Now I've missed it. Passed.

Space has adopted me, the unknown orphan
who so soon seeks to run away.
(What's so enticing out in space?)

Before shooting out too far,
my direction, I succeed in changing
—don't inquire how, it's only a dream
        in space, anarchist realm in an overly ordered void.

Salmon, swimming strokes I improvise on the spot
        (swimming laps, running laps
        —is there a difference here?),
I manage to draw nearer the planet I thought lost.

And in time, on cue, gravity reversed, I see blue.
I'm falling free through air
concerned with nothing except for...

                    There!

That land mass on a cloud,
it appears to be a copy of an old town
from the time of our country's founding
near the shores, long, long ag—

wait

Upon landing, the grass, green, yes,
but not living. Not any higher
than the hair standing up on my arm.
The town itself is silent, deadly.
Not even a breeze haunts the roads.
The dirt is loose, unpacked, undisturbed;
   I feel warmed by the solitary charm.

The quaintness doesn't elude me,
with shops and houses made of…
what? This material is not known to me,
like a mixture of waxy metals from planets far off.

Well, I'm nearer the stars; accept these strange things.
I know no foe will reach these heavens; here, no fiend shall sing.

My heaven is my den, where I alone will walk
and contemplate the ways of those fallen, left below.

❖

I'm at a crossroads (actually,
the town hall in the town's square),

and encountering a tocsin
while noticing the bell's still.

The nighttime tales portend future events—
subtle, but sure, and soon to fly.
Somewhere in the shadows
a council sits, calculating,
analyzing the past to interpret the future.

I realize this before the waking hours—
I'm finally steps ahead!
This courthouse to which I have been led
may provide the answers I dread.

Spontaneous, unpredictable, I shun the front door,
and leap up to a windowsill on the second floor.

And I was deceived! The second floor is nonexistent
before and below. I peer out and down into the abyss
and jump forward, feet first, to find my destiny.

❖

A black fog, a silver mist, enshrouds all around.
So I imagine a staff—my crutch, altered—
matching my height, to feel my way about.

Twirling and poking, on the tips of my toes,
    whirling and twirling,
        who will take whom by surprise?

I feel their breaths, something pulsating…
My pursuers have me discovered…
Or have I discovered a lair of theirs?

An arena, in truth, I see between gaps
in the mist that form as it rises to the supposed second level,
which does exist, in fact, I see now, as a balcony
that circles, touching all six sixty degrees.
I can only make out eyes, hair, and paraphernalia—
enough to relieve me, seeing some others there.
A double relief to make out the colors
as matching those sported by my allies on the battlefields below.
Others wear white—gowns or robes.And these opposing gangs
rival in percentages fifty to fifty.

I scream up to them for answers,
but: Guess what? No sound,
no replies coming forth…but still
the darkness moves around.
And slowly some mist fades grey, then white,
then forms, in human shape, my first reply.

From behind a tree, with which this arena floor is forested,
emerges a girl with sunny-honey-golden hair,
      bearing a sword at her side,
wearing a smile stretching wide. She stares ice through my soul
      as my breath condenses, "Lora"
—the name of the being this apparition mocks.

She nods in acknowledgment of the name, her name, my fear.
Among a forested range, a premature playground,
what is she doing here?

    Doing where? Share the care. In your games, nothing's fair.

Reading my thoughts, she answers,
in riddles, ciphered through.

    Where to run, bounce away? You've slipped, dipped into the fray.
        A staff—you're armed. To harm me?
      Wish you may, wish you might, stay and play
          —fight!

She swings her sword at my neck,
by instinct, I twirl my staff, deflect.
Step backward, and ask: "What the hell
has infected you?"

I am your Love, first in your heart,
one you can't kill, live with, or with part.
I'll haunt you from here till the end,
rend your papery heart, lovefriend;
you're too much the coward to run backward.

Spittle lit, she swipes again,
misses my throat, but nicks my chin,
laughs with glee at each drop,
then lunges for my heart.

Now's no time to be cautious;
take the risk as she passes,
trip her up and grab her arm
and toss her to the ground.

She's not distanced, but disarmed.
Among the "boos," my allies cheer on
up in the stands; the silence is up,
now broken.

I take her sword, toss it in the trees,
she begins to fade, coming to her knees,
laughing still, giggling on
and on, and on…

Among the claps and cheers,
barks and boos,
the forest trees shed to columns.
The audience remains the same
in this arena, auditorium.

No forest—it is as if
I'm under spotlights on a stage.

> *Don't sweat or cry,*
> *don't be amazed;*
> *you're so used to changing shades.*
> *Be a man. Up your age.*
> *Withdraw? Why not be engaged?*

Krystina fades in in her right
from behind a column,
under her own spotlight.
Sunset-red hair, temper flared,
and her flaming blade.

I ready my staff, brace my stance,
"Krystina…"

> *I know, you hate to dance;*
> *you hate to get involved,*
> *solve any snowy mysteries…*

She swings and sings, I block and turn.
She can't cut quick, but my arm is burned.
I yell. She grins. Above, her friends
stamp and cheer an ovation.

I stumble over while she bows;
I grab her ankle, trip her down.
On the ground, she swings for me;
I roll out of her lane,
hop to my feet, turn for my staff,
tossed over when my arm went bad;
it now lies by the edge, where
the columns stand, stout and thick.
To the point, almost there,
I fall on my face, look up to see
a violet-clad, dark-haired girl
bearing no smile, just a smirk.

Who's the fool, Circled Jerk?
In these shadows, Know-It-All lurks…

Shanna's foot on my staff,
five feet away; she beckons me.
I crawl backward,
not wanting to meet her sword

in this arena, on this site,
transformed once more:
a sandy ground
of stairs and mirrors,
striped lights,
defying natural boundaries.

Bounds, of course, you must know;
a small man in body and scope
of mind. B and M condemned
to wallow in a pit.

On my feet, I turn to run,
but with the force of a cannon,
kick to my chest, a black boot worn
by my new foe. "Shawna!"

No blacker dog lives in Hell.
My luck—I tried to like, dispel
the curse within you,
but you forced it into me!

With a vengeance, no love lost,
she swings and swipes, kicks and flips.
Who knew one so dull on the eyes
could defy gravity so beautifully?

Nearby, Shanna leads the cheers
and jeers of the circling crowd above.
Standing on my staff, spiked
baton twirling in her hand,
sword to her side, Shanna derides
while Shawna keeps, keeps on trying
to take my heart or head,
slice me seven ways dead.

To duck and dodge with turns and flips,
wearies me; soon she won't miss.
I pull a trick, surprise with this:
sand tossed at her eyes.

She recoils, but lands a kick
down below, drawing out stars.
Another kick in the face—
to my back; I'm future waste.
Deathblow, oncoming,
she lunges happily for it.

Then a thought kisses me:
sword in my hand,
instantly,

lifted to my feet,
smiling.

A fair fight, now?

"Shut up, you cow."
I engage Shawna, not knowing how,
but not unlike a swordmaster,
I counter every try of hers.

Still on defense, the crowd intense,
strobe lights, turned on, begin to flick,
reflecting off the mirrors,
working to my disadvantage.

She gets cocky, swings for my head;
cocksure more, I slash her stomach instead.
She doubles over, lets out a howl
and comes up wearing a broad scowl,
stripped clean of black jacket, jeans;
cornrows gone, hair flowing free;
shapely build; face smooth, not coarse;
lovely, hazel eyes,
yet somehow barren;
my never-and-now
nightmare—Charynn.

Gleaming swords in both of her hands,
the blue lights flicker, beating as
my heart goes faster, faster,
cheating (O, Master),
skipping beats,
stopping, stuttering, amplified,
as the surroundings follow suit,
changing constantly, outside and in.
Rivals, curious seekers, friends,
allies, would-be lovers.
Blind from the mind:
a black mask, my face, covers.
This coliseum, this stadium, this pit,
this amphitheater, this arena
—the climax, this is it.

> *Yes, so we come down to this,*
> *here, quagmired in your abyss.*
> *No words to say, we've had our day,*
> *the letters won't connect.*
> *You wear the mask, guilty conscience,*
> *it spells your fear, doom pronounces*
> *till death due you; for the girls who*
> *still feel and cry and hope to die—*
> *let's make this wish your own!*

Like a flurry or whirlwind, she comes at me
with blinding speed. My sword counters
each and every, and yet, she still draws blood
from the pores on my forehead, on one wrist,
on my chest—I don't feel her blade but still
she makes nicks and cuts and stabs
my left side. I can't go down…it's not the end…

"I own this town!"

I heal myself with a thought—
invincible, invulnerable,
impervious to pain, to her words,
to her slurs, to her swords, to all feelings,
to (not the least) remorse.

Those who are defensive sink away;
offensive ones succeed by play.
I swallow hard, shout "en garde!"
and charge at her like a fool.
She easily maintains her cool—no sweat,
no struggle. No sympathy from me.
Slash one wrist—she shrieks—
In that blind moment, take her head!

But I blinked (am I blood-shy?);
she disappeared
when I shut my eyes.
And now I'm all one,
one lonely,
enraged: "Bars or bones,
I'll break your cage!"

Darkness

silence

then the flicks.
Strobing lights begin again;
mirrors and columns reappear
—a mishmash of the scenes.

Alone no more. Emerging from
mirrors, they—one all—come:
Lora, Krystina,
Shanna, Shawna,
Charynn.
Each bearing carpers' swords;
each bearing sharpened words.

The five encircle me,
at star points; the design,
if connected by straight lines,
would form a hateful pentagram.
The vultures circle—grimaces
and grins spreading wide…
Forget this—
The time is mine!
I slice and slash, thrust and parry;
they deflect, growing madder,
and yet, appearing merry.
In their offense, they come
forward, singing:

> *Timid, coward, lie in dreams,*
> *absorb pain, hold in screams.*

> *Act shy as you will*
> *but your curtain falls tonight.*
> *Apathetic beyond shame,*

the one who gave shame its name!

> *Task your masks,*

duck and dodge,
play your games and act your roles.

A selfish man with petty cares,
change your shade and camouflage.

All those you've wronged

and defiled

come clean,
drown black back to brown.

Yes, you've set a better trap
in your game of rats and cats;
milksop

flip, flop

stunned stunts

can't develop true personalities;
that is why you don the masks

party-of-one
party at home

party to my murder! Come!

You spoke no words and I died!
What in hell is your alibi?

Fabrics of reality enter dreams to tie me.
Phases, phase in, phase out; I will wake up
and rip apart these lies.

"Lies," you think, are our words?
The Prince of Lies himself's disturbed!

One will come in latter,
better days

to dance

around
your head on a lance!

Confront your ghosts and demons now
to avoid the fate—

kiss and kill!

You can't compete, competitor,
you even stoop to cheat
on equal leveled

> *playing fields,*
> *false start, false heart—*
> *Attack!*

And on and on and on it went; it seems
several hours were spent.
They came and went behind their columns
and disappeared when I cut close.

The above crowd, at fever pitch,
screamed and yelled, stomped and cheered.
Intense emotions, the arena quaked,
the air thundered, the lights but blinked
until
the ringleader,
Charynn, face-to-face,
taunts:

> *Jellyfish free-swimming in dreams,*
> *can't help but to lie*

I swing—
she blinks out,
reappears at my side.

Dreams, the repercussions of a life lived
in the shadows, shades fruit trees give,
separate from reality, truth and consequences.

I prepare to strike, but I'm not blind;
one has snuck up from behind. On a foot I spin,
slash through. The body falls in a heap.

The crowd stills, freezes;
statues stoned.
For one moment, I'm all alone
in blood-flooding lights
—no laughter, no bodies
but that of Felicity's
at my feet. My sword,
I drop. I follow
on my knees.
Here come the sobs,
here comes the breeze…
no—
crimson snow,
the only weather to show
what I dare not say
but what my diseased heart knows.

From her severed head, I take a lock of hair
and hold it to my heart. The tears are here.
The creeping fear

the sun breaks

I awake

UNHAPPY QUESTIONS

Crimson snow,
icy sickles, and windy hauntings—
winter life boasts free spirits from ages passed.
History has taught me white is Heaven, as is snow
if it's pure.

Covered grass,
bush skeletons, and ashen sunglow—
from the fall, Hell's born, disguised, but chilling still.
Nature's lessons drew this one into the nurses' class
for a cure.

I raised my hand for an answer
to questions, to this cancer
solving tissues, high
feasting on whatever's clean, white, unseen, within,
drinking dry fluids in order to fill, begin
the lowest dive.

I asked some god for one answer
to questions, to this dance or
foreign ritual
with stomps, twirls, and rattles playing out in my skull,

performed by adolescent brown mimes, though dull,
happy to live.

No reply,
acknowledgment, or even a glance—
nature's nurses care nothing for those far-gone,
beyond the pale. No saviors are coming to surprise.
So why wait?

All one, all,
blackening skies, and freezing breezes—
not much time until the beatings cease for good,
those in the chest and on the breast: words stronger than fists.
Moral weight.

My sun has yet to rise, answer
questions about this stance, poor,
taken behind eyes:
submitting all I have to give to an unknown,
three-blind gamble for an existence still unshown.
In hand, five knives.

FISHING,
WITH CLIPPED WINGS
(FELICITY'S THEME)

Superstition blasts the minds of men
in mazes, lost in their own ways,
foolishly floundering about as grounded fish
wondering in their last gasps
about the questions (who cares for answers?)
of love and life, intimacy and
—No matter. For this one, I've descended
to lure, shatter his glass tank
of laughing gas.

Who says immaculate women can't change boys into men?
Did not God create Eve to convert Adam,
and Mary to fleece the Prince's wounded pride?
(With a baptism by candles,
an immersion in a pool of white wine...)

He speaks to me of God living within some,
self-righteous talk, blighting meanings of freedom.
"No one has the right to be wrong,"
I answer him with love
for my Lord
and my Savior.

My seduction into the arms of an angel,
holy spirit lifting me above and beyond the clouds
of confusion and man's false reasoning,
showed me the true path of liberty to sunned beauty.

His seduction away from selfish arrogance
shall raise him up into a humble man, a sincere servant
of the Master in the paradise devoid of oppression,
devil impressionists, idle lies, and carrion for idols.

I offered a sacrifice, as was my duty;
now I offer another in order to dry out
this body. I'd imbibed and fell close
to intoxication, but those visions never quit me…

He speaks of some sovereign entity,
makes motions proclaiming an identity.
I've offered him the love I've seen written of.

How does he expect to reach Heaven
unless he come through me?

THE WAY IT SLOWS

In younger days, this thinking went without saying:
Love is the most devastating sickness,
an illness rivaling cancer
running at hyperspeed,
sinking a lover's cells,
making a concert
of blues-playing,
non-singing
orange prisoners.

Losing myself in a quicker mire
than the one that sired Adam,
I became a young man
without a soul, a Thomas,
a twin to an essence
of sin, doubt-delving
ever-deeper within
for comforting skin.

> Haters think this is how love goes
> —but do summers sleep in snow?
> Deserts think this is where streams flow—
> but can blind girls paint rainbows?

Non sequiturs come
and quit me.
This is a mad dress well suited
for one not thought about
during the act,
ill-considered
after the fact,
spat out naked,
kicked around in rags,
running in circles,
playing marked-man's tag.

Parents bitterly rent their souls
—but can diamonds burn like coals?
Serve a dessert made out of hearts—
but can Happiness come apart?

My mind now just like a mud pie…
Can an idea, never born, die?

Crazy—love—death—
Where's the save, Dove?
What, raised with lies,
falls in Love?

YEAR EIGHT

PANACEA

He said the words most distressed girls want to hear.
He said the words most men are wont to swallow.
    Though yet to receive a ring,
        I have prepared the dowry:
An ablution by candlelight under the glow of a honeyed moon.

I told him of a disease that is mixed, flows with the blood;
aided by the heart, it imbues the soul.
    Well, perhaps he misconstrued
        only melancholy moods.
No matter. Out of loving lies come binding truths.

Prior engagements shall be postponed
until I snatch this heathen out from his own.
    Captured wolf—set him free,
        cured-pure of injuries;
his silence will respond to Hell's call, praise me.

All the cares and woes surrounding him
shall be tied in nets, raised, cast to the heavens.
    In this mind-state, can he
    forge ahead, peacefully,
squinting to see—through breaths condensed—destiny.

He said the words that thinly veil blue lyrics.
He said the words that belie his happiness.
  I refuse to stand unnamed,
    tolerate a war that's claimed
a man's sanity, promising to end in grey ashes.

I told him I knew of his true point of origin,
studied esoteric topics in my spare time.
  I empathize with the stress
    felt by those who think they're less
than what they would be, if only born in a cleaner setting.

As for the man who thinks he is mine,
or vice versa, is he false fruit on the vine?
  I need to rid myself
    of it all. Think of Health—
mental, physical: the rungs a soul must climb.

All those boys before were just God's tests;
my introduction to Sevin proves I'm blessed.
  I could, before mobs thick,
    perform a magic trick.
But why share him? I'm the one whose heart is sick.

F O O L   C I R C L E

Magdalena
whirls in her tomb
while the girl, who would be ticking
from her womb, twists and turns,
expecting me to take a leap.
          I'm relegated to the audience.
Begotten, I forgot this,
longing for the honeyed rays of the spotlight
illuminating the stage,
giving it the appearance of a pond
or a Clowns' Pool.

She's the swan, graceful,
garbed all in white.
But just like everyone else,
her moves unpave waves
and the waters ripple outward,
          outward,

        wining
       in circles.

I was invited
to attend this masquerade, front-row seat
for the opening ceremony marked by a ballet.
The main festivities to come later:
the drinking, dancing, and midnight unmasking…
But
the revelations of faces behind covers
can cause fools to trip into their own pooled aspirations
or to bumble, babbling, into built-up hopes,
crumbling something that might have towered.

The polluted airs have mutated arms
that pull at me, embrace me—
Me, facing all the boys
that have come
and gone
before

                    …wrong number,
                        whatever it is.

DANCE OF THE SWORDS

See? We agree fault doesn't lie with me,
but you, slithering, wrapping poles all these years.
Perhaps you didn't hear, waxed with stupidity or fear;
tearing airs, I guess some gases mixed you up.
I know seducers slinking on missions.
No need for that with upstanding men.
A woman and a boy
resting under different shades—
How nice now to hear words of truth!
(Since both blades are drawn, be on guard.)

The fragrance of fools—what, tell, could smell more foul
than a man unwashed in holy waters?
The perfume of conceit takes to women and repels
men familiar with the musk and what it masks.
With no blood-ties, your future is as dust—
Dust hit by the rain as long as there's pain.
As mud, I can stand firm,
packed, unyielding to the winds—
Stepped on, kicked in blind men's parades.
Enjoy your warm welcome in Hell.

You people have played this headhunt game throughout time,
proselytizing to the poor among my kind.
My people are not common with those deviants
out only for pleasure or to get rich.
Why examine from afar, keep questions last?
A student unprepared to learn singed facts…
Your kind brags of God
made in your own self-image, while I—
Prefer I prostrate before an image of you?
Bow out now, 'less your neck is thick.

I'll only bow to One; you will, too, when the ghost comes
to haunt you in the dreams you brought to life.
A mad mistress who conjures demons with a wish,
or a modern woman spooked by goblins?
And to you, life is a fairy tale?
What else when dealing with girls who won't grow?
So my sin is ego, but
what does your mirror show?
Rays of emotions from a white soul,
not a wrapped carcass with a black heart.

Not a queen of hearts, perhaps a temptress princess,
pale serpent hidden under scales of sequins.
Short-sighted in the mind as well as eyes; the history

of heathenism is intertwined with your line.
Your perceptions are freckled with large spots.
I believe that most can shed off their past.
But you lie intimate
by the tracks of those men...
You speak in silver tongues, forked,
like the roads I've run. From now, I'll walk.

Why pace yourself now? Aren't you known to shoot quick
and run panting with the others in the pack—
Out chasing cats? I see how you can assume that
with your dogmatic world-views, grand delusions.
It's a curse that you're doomed to black fate.
Unlike you, I don't have leprosy.
All cults resist the cures
for the venoms that swell their ranks.
To whom do you look to cure you of hate?
My condolences—your race is lost.

It's a similar race we run, out from shrouds into the sun.
A chasm prevents us from truly relating.
Love bridges gaps, far and wide, of various depths,
but bridges are useless unless one crosses them.
I'd a past, chained, sheltered. Never again.
I never offered to show you those graves.

Why must I be blamed
for wanting us joined in Paradise?
You take your god, I'll keep my life.
A farewell kiss—Goodbye, damned witch.

(Farewell to my years of youth;
harmony devolves to scratchy discord:
Living in a cage of gold and grey steel
built by song-strong men who don't feel
all the combined lives they disrupt.
Greetings to my mature truth;
broken lies are all they note and record:
Going to accord, spread smiles of malice
on peaceful faces, forced callous,
insured by dry hearts, sunned bankrupt.)

WHITE FROST, BLACK ROSE

Dwelling on second-handed lifelines,
framed, incarcerated in still-times—
this is where my conscience flies to run and play.
Thinking of some liberal nights' zeal
and how imprisoned spirits must feel
when the world stops turning just short of yawning day...

I sampled freely with blue moon-dyes,
buying the lies about the sun's lies.
What could that be? Naked Felicity? Opaque
bedroom walls. None of them mine. I sense
another twin, soulmate. Skull too dense
to think or see...Heart replaces brain, speeds to break.

No ribbons. No ties. Just a surprise:
the white frost on a black rose
before the sun comes and what's there evaporates.
The thirsty rose cries for the late sun
but freezes in anticipation.
Hidden love half-expressed, spurned, worm-turns into hate.

Mirrors' errors inflamed the heart's ache;
to ease, impaled with wooden mistakes.

Pleasing plans went awry, lighting my soul aflame.
　　　To palliate, I palled with black guilt
　　　the coffin, a body sum-luck built,
but ghosts came to claim the senses of one misnamed.

　　　Bloodflow ceased—essential assistant.
　　　Sweat? Tears? Who to kid? Nonexistent.
Streams would imply my emotion returned as new.
　　　In truth, the ill absence had removed
　　　what I was blind to: true loves, truths loved.
A fate due, deserved. Fall away from mercy's view.

The beat dies; one melody lies like
　　　the white frost on a black rose
after clouds descend in the pre-dawn shroud of night.
Before the sun can shine a wake-up,
the chill steals, preventing the make-up.
The heart shivers, shrivels, drained by a parasite.

LAMENTATIONS
OF THE TREES

Why is it said that leaves
do not fall at midnight?
Would it be a turn too taboo?
Or is it just due
to the stillness of the winds?
Or is this tale even true?

Oak, or mahogany—
What is the real difference to me?
Are they still not beautiful trees,
  known for durability,
  known to withstand the brunts of the worst?
They bear no relation to me.

A brilliant full moon
with rings, rosy,
a blushing complexion…
Should I feel such displacement?
Should I feel at all?
The daystar was my halo—
How did I come to be banished
to the asylum for the audience?

See? Never mind the flock.
See how, when one falls,
it is a solitary dive?
The winds cleave stems from limbs by day,
blow a course a little ways,
then leave you for midnight.

Piles of discarded figments of a fig tree
that grew in a warm region set aside
solely for me and my soulmate.

Single. Locked out
by the Seventh Gate.

EPILOGUE

AUTUMN THEMES

How many faces can a man wear
before he wears himself out?
Inquiries such as these find their answers in my tracks.
Therapeutic recounting of a sorrowful chapter
may, if not close the chasm,
perhaps still (will ill) phantasmic spasms.

A lesson learned by enduring a passage
decorated—or littered—with leaves
varying in hues and sizes,
shapes and vein patterns.
These leaves, now long fallen and dry,
can be judged by nothing
but a discriminating eye.

All too familiar. Not unlike young life,
when rhymes of nurseries reign, yet reason's unborn.
Never mind the corridors and phantoms in their heads;
concern yourself with nothing but the passage you tread.
Is it not in the nature of man
              to act capriciously?
Is it not in the nature of woman
              to do no less the same?

With just a solitary torch to aid a lone traveler down
the twists and turns of a cavern, still unmeasured through,
who else should he meet but the shadowy friends and family
of the fallen hero left back at the entrance—
How to explain to them the child is no more,
and why the lone one wears his clothes?

The once proud torch flickers to fade (as it was bound to do),
owing its fate to the jostling of the congregation
and their babble, unrefined.
One struggles to get away
and succeeds in finding himself damned to darkness.

Imagine a life centered in the situation as recounted.

Imagine the joy one felt when entering the exit!

He'd gone from riding, running,
walking (tripped) to crawling—
his only means to escape
to the rays he'd thought lost.

Now he comes by again, with shrouded memories,
to leave them in a forgotten orchard's tomb,
guarded only by sticks
and one stone.

A ghost moving
from misogynist
to mourning Eve?
Well, that's another story
to divorce
from Heaven's familiar Hell.

Today, I'm just passing through.

NOTES

THE SYNOPSIS

Before kissing off his hometown for good, Sevin walks through it one last time, reminiscing about the experiences that pushed him from Childhood and carried him through Adolescence.

His recollections begin with grade five and Lora, the first girl who made him fall in love at first sight. Nine-year-old Sevin is not exactly poor, but the ten-year-old girl is from the much better side of the tracks. With the differences in status, skin color, age, and who knows what else, Sevin realizes she is unattainable, and he gets his first bitter taste of how irrational and unfair life can be.

In grade six, Sevin and his classmates are the seniors of elementary school, the top dogs. But, again, he realizes not all are equal as he becomes cognizant of how the popular obtain and maintain their popularity, and how the rules are different for boys and girls. In the pecking order, he may as well be a mutt. A new girl, Krystina, pulls his attention, but he maintains his distance. Krystina has an abusive boyfriend, and it may be Sevin's empathy that accounts for his deep attraction to her. When the girl dies, Sevin's guilt almost overwhelms him as he wonders if he could have said or done something to prevent the tragedy.

The entry into junior high school brings another shift as Sevin's elementary-school friends break their ties with him, an all-too-obvious outcast. As he struggles to find new friends, things get worse at home. His alcoholic mother and his older sister verbally and psychologically bully him to the point where he attempts suicide. The only other female Sevin notices during this trying time is Karen, a girl who is only at the school temporarily and, in style and behavior, seemingly out of place, as if she's something ethereal. Something about her odd presence encourages Sevin to turn inward, going deeper than he's ever gone before. He becomes determined to live on and proactively engage in this little-world war called Adolescence. But he's not quite ready yet. For the remainder of the year, he resolves to remain in the blackground, studying, until he determines his appropriate role.

There is only so much blending a black kid can do in a predominantly white and conservative town. The experiences of the previous three years have gone down like bitter medicine; how could he not eventually lash out? By grade eight, Sevin has become a short-tempered bully. Shawna, a new girl in town, takes notice. Also an African-American, she determines that the two of them become an item. Unknown to Sevin, her motives have nothing to do with love. Shawna believes the self-destructive behavior of a minority is not a good look in the eyes of the majority, so she tries in her small way to reform Sevin by giving him something he never had: a legitimate girlfriend. Not being physically attracted to her, Sevin is hesitant at first, but Shawna plays every psychological trick she can to steer him into her arms. It works, for a while. When Sevin finally grows tired of her, he is psychologically worse than before. He begins to concoct schemes that will land him girls that are prettier and more popular than Shawna, and he ends his relationship with her in one of the most despicable ways a boy can.

The little-big world of high school will soon be his—so Sevin has determined before entering grade nine. He figures his key to popularity and any girl he wants is to become an athlete. He joins the track team and soon becomes a star runner…but only as part of a relay team. He wants to be a superstar on his own. In the meantime, as part of a winning team, he begins catching many girls' attention. Felicity, the leader of the school's Bible study group, is among them. She sees a damaged soul and wants to capture it, saving it and earning herself major points in Heaven. She also catches Sevin's eye; she's one of the most beautiful—and innocent—girls he's ever seen. The two knew each other early in elementary school, but they'd taken different paths. Sevin now does what he can to reconnect, operating on immature and barely coherent theories on love, no decent or mature philosophy. Felicity, following a similarly immature philosophy of "flirty fishing," plays hard-to-get, frustrating Sevin.

During the summer vacation between their freshman and sophomore years, Felicity does volunteer work while Sevin goes upstate to track camp. His only goal is to become a faster runner, one who can win long-distance races solo; he doesn't expect to meet a gorgeous girl by the name of Charynn who happens to be faster than him. She's not only African-American, but also a black separatist. When she's not racing against or hooking up with him, Charynn schools Sevin on "hidden" black history and the importance of blacks sticking together. He is in the palms of her hands. When he returns to school for his sophomore year, he wants little to do with Felicity or any other girl. His heart belongs to Charynn, and his thoughts belong to his new ideology.

But Felicity is no quitter, not when her and Sevin's souls are at stake. Felicity also harbors secrets: an on-again-off-again boyfriend, and an on-again-off-again affinity for wine. Sevin is a conversion project she's sure will help cure her of both problems. She persuades him to become her study partner for history class, intending to use their studying sessions to persuade him to choose her version of Christianity over his version of black nationalism, and to choose her over any other girl. It's not easy, but she uses every trick in her book. Sevin eventually cuts off all communication with Charynn.

Sevin and Felicity get even more serious in their junior year. During another study session at her house, Felicity experiences a bout of delirium and leads Sevin to believe she has mysterious but fatal illness. Shocked and feeling helpless, Sevin has a vivid dream in which all of his significant crushes and "loves" confront him. It's a violent attack of his subconscious, and Sevin survives the battle with an epiphany: Felicity was right about him and his soul; she must be the only female he can truly love, the only one who can save him. Emerging from a period of something like delirium himself, Sevin—in "love" and out of regret for his past actions—vows to do anything and everything to make Felicity's remaining days joyful, while saving his own soul in the process.

His senior year brings another devastating shock when Sevin learns Felicity's secrets. Her problem with alcohol bitterly reminds him of his mother's addiction, and her flirty-fishing habits with numerous boys over the years disgusts him, even as he barely acknowledges the fact he's engaged in very similar behavior over the years for even more selfish reasons. The absolute worst, however, is his discovery that Felicity is planning to marry her secret on-again-off-again boyfriend, the same boy who saved her long ago when she was a totally lost soul. Once she was saved, she had tried to pay the blessings forward; with at least one boy, it didn't end well; Sevin was initially intended to be a do-over.

Discovering all of this, Sevin loses it and confronts Felicity, who also loses it. The two have a knock-down-drag-out argument before parting ways. Unknown to Sevin, Felicity truly was falling in love with him and considering telling her boyfriend to kiss off for good as she believed Sevin (possibly) to be her true soulmate; but, in utter sadness, she realizes she's probably lost him forever. As for Sevin, his soul and psyche have been damaged almost beyond repair. He fears what awaits him as he leaves high school to enter the greater world.

Yet, somehow, the present-day Sevin has found redemption. The story of that transformation is something he'll dwell on some other time. For now, he's moving on, leaving all these memories buried—he prays.

ABOUT THE AUTHOR

Harambee Grey-Sun is a poet and metaphysical/speculative fiction writer. The word best describing his work is "dark." He uses elements of fantasy, horror, noir, and science fiction to spin bizarre, mind-bending, and (some might say) heretical tales that explore the meaning of identity and the nature of consciousness. His poetry has appeared in a handful of literary journals, including *CrossConnect*, *Epicenter*, *RiverSedge*, the *South Carolina Review*, and the *Wisconsin Review*. He is also an alumnus of the Community of Writers at Squaw Valley.

FURTHER READING

Want to read more of the author's poetry?
Enter the HyperVerse: www.nextpoet.net

www.ingramcontent.com/pod-product-compliance
Lightning Source LLC
LaVergne TN
LVHW051056080426
835508LV00019B/1899